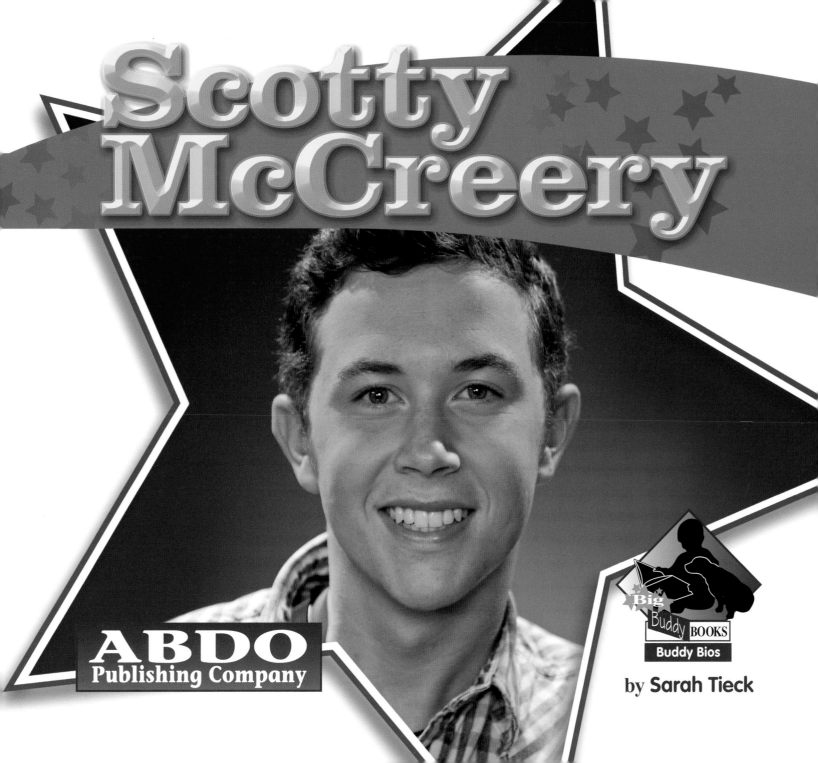

Scotty McCreery

ABDO
Publishing Company

Big Buddy BOOKS
Buddy Bios

by **Sarah Tieck**

VISIT US AT

www.abdopublishing.com

Published by ABDO Publishing Company, PO Box 398166, Minneapolis, MN 55439.

Printed in the United States of America, North Mankato, Minnesota.
102011
012012

 PRINTED ON RECYCLED PAPER

Coordinating Series Editor: Rochelle Baltzer
Contributing Editors: Megan M. Gunderson, BreAnn Rumsch, Marcia Zappa
Graphic Design: Maria Hosley
Cover Photograph: *AP Photo*: Jeff Christensen.
Interior Photographs/Illustrations: *AP Photo*: AP Photo (p. 9), Michael Becker/Fox/PictureGroup via AP IMAGES (p. 13), Mark Davis/Fox/PictureGroup via AP IMAGES (pp. 5, 15, 18), Richard Drew (p. 15), Paul Drinkwater/ NBC/NBCU Photo Bank via AP Images (p. 15), Peter Kramer/NBC/NBCU Photo Bank via AP Images (p. 29), Mercury Nashville/19 Recordings/Interscope Recordings (p. 21), Frank Micelotta/FOX/PictureGroup via AP IMAGES (pp. 7, 8, 10, 25), Chris Pizzello (p. 19), Disney, Matt Stroshane (p. 27); *Getty Images*: Robert Willett/ Raleigh News & Observer/MCT via Getty Images (p. 23); *PictureGroup*: Michael Becker/Fox (p. 17).

Library of Congress Cataloging-in-Publication Data

Tieck, Sarah, 1976-
  Scotty McCreery : American idol winner / Sarah Tieck.
    p. cm. -- (Big buddy biographies)
  ISBN 978-1-61783-227-7
  1. McCreery, Scotty, 1993---Juvenile literature. 2. Singers--United States--Biography--Juvenile literature. I. Title.
  ML3930.M375T54 2012
  782.421642092--dc23
  [B]
                            2011041513

Scotty
McCreery

Contents

Rising Star 4

Family Ties 6

Growing Up 8

First Steps 12

Star Makers 14

American Idol 16

First Album 20

A Singer's Life 22

Off the Stage 26

Buzz 28

Snapshot 30

Important Words 31

Web Sites 31

Index 32

Rising Star

Scotty McCreery is a talented singer. He is best known as an *American Idol* winner. In 2011, he won the tenth season of the popular television show.

Scotty sings country music. He is known for his deep voice.

5

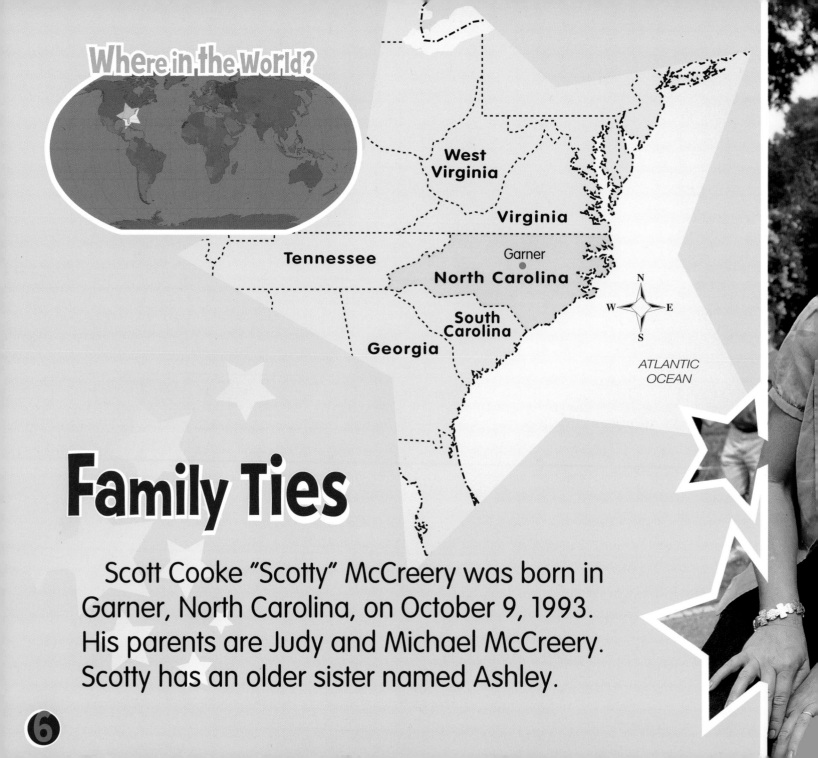

West Virginia

Virginia

Tennessee

Garner

North Carolina

South Carolina

Georgia

ATLANTIC OCEAN

N W E S

Family Ties

Scott Cooke "Scotty" McCreery was born in Garner, North Carolina, on October 9, 1993. His parents are Judy and Michael McCreery. Scotty has an older sister named Ashley.

Scotty's parents are very proud of his success. They often attend events with him.

Growing Up

Scotty has always loved music. People noticed his talent when he sang Elvis Presley songs as a young child. Scotty also sang in a church **choir**. And, he learned to play **guitar** when he was ten years old.

Did you know...

Scotty went to Timber Drive Elementary School in Garner. His teachers say he was friendly and polite.

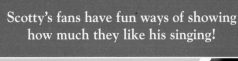

Scotty's fans have fun ways of showing how much they like his singing!

Elvis Presley was one of Scotty's childhood heroes. Elvis became a famous singer in the 1950s. Many people call him the King of Rock and Roll.

9

Did you know...

Scotty played Conrad Birdie in *Bye Bye Birdie*. This character was modeled after Elvis Presley!

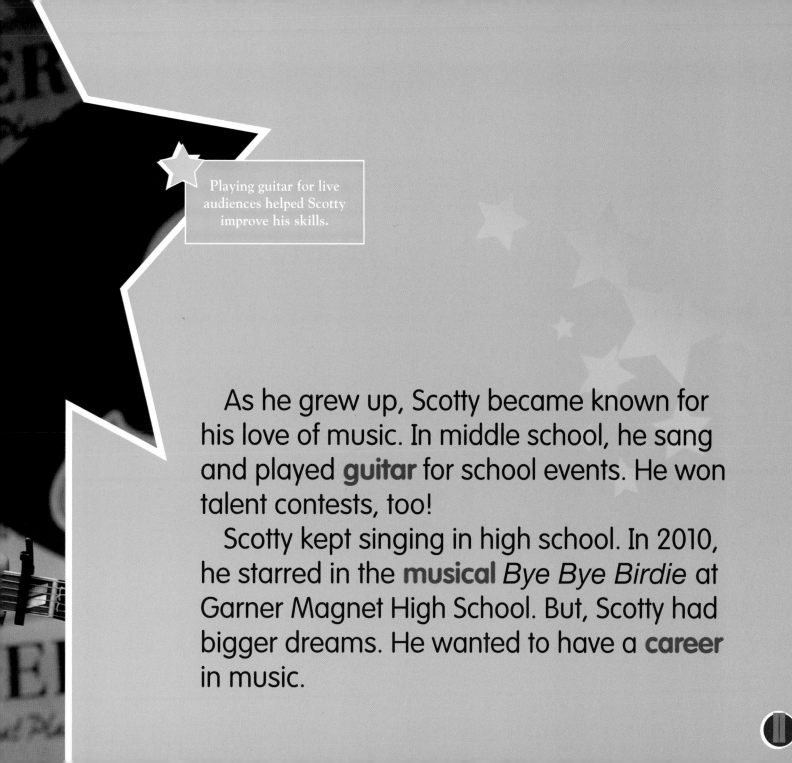

Playing guitar for live audiences helped Scotty improve his skills.

As he grew up, Scotty became known for his love of music. In middle school, he sang and played **guitar** for school events. He won talent contests, too!

Scotty kept singing in high school. In 2010, he starred in the **musical** *Bye Bye Birdie* at Garner Magnet High School. But, Scotty had bigger dreams. He wanted to have a **career** in music.

First Steps

In summer 2010, Scotty auditioned for *American Idol*. He didn't tell many people he was going to try out.

Judges Randy Jackson, Jennifer Lopez, and Steven Tyler were surprised by Scotty's deep voice. Scotty was very happy when he made it to the next round!

Scotty sang "Your Man" by Josh Turner at his audition. Josh is one of Scotty's heroes.

Star Makers

American Idol is a popular television show. Each season, talented singers **compete** to be named the next American Idol.

Many singers find success after leaving the show. Some go on to record albums or **release** songs. A few have even won **Grammy Awards**! Others appear in movies or television shows.

David Cook won *American Idol* in 2008. Scotty sang one of David's songs at his eighth grade graduation.

Kelly Clarkson won the first season of *American Idol* in 2002.

Carrie Underwood won *American Idol* in 2005. She sings country music, like Scotty!

American Idol

Scotty made it all the way through the *American Idol* tryouts! He was one of the top 13 finalists on the show. That winter, he lived in California for the taping of the show.

Each week, Scotty sang and **competed** on television. He learned a lot about being a better **performer**.

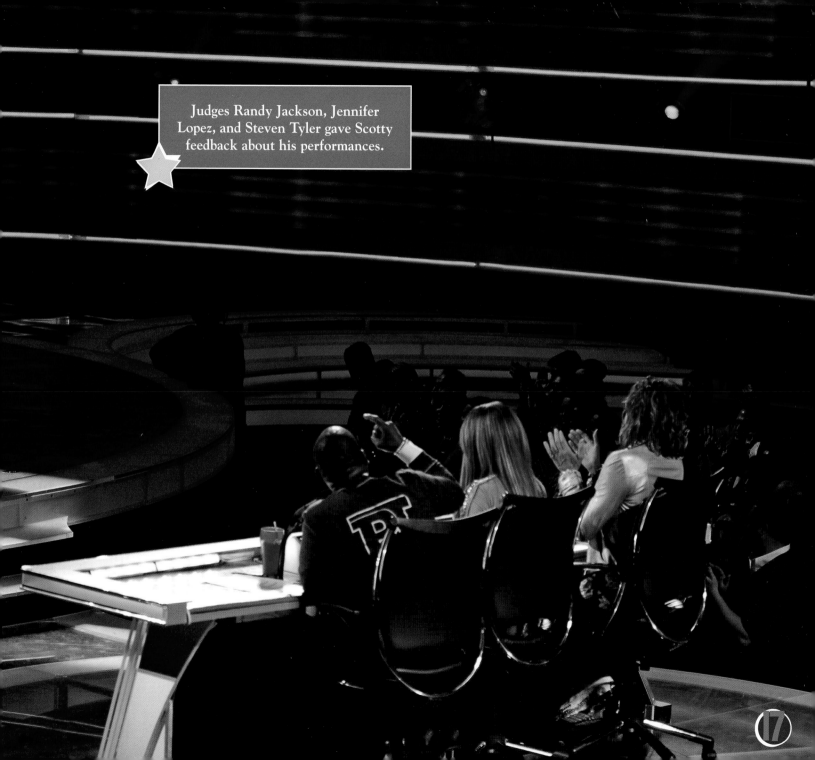

Judges Randy Jackson, Jennifer Lopez, and Steven Tyler gave Scotty feedback about his performances.

Scotty sang with country star Tim McGraw during the *American Idol* finale.

In May 2011, Scotty and Lauren Alaina were the last two singers left. They were excited to see who would win *American Idol*. After singing "I Love You This Big," Scotty won. He was thrilled!

Scotty was so happy when he won that he cried onstage.

First Album

After winning *American Idol*, Scotty worked hard to record an album. In October 2011, his first album came out. It is called *Clear As Day*. Scotty included songs he felt were true to his life and beliefs.

Scotty's album has country music songs. Some of them are about his belief in God.

SCOTTY McCREERY

CLEAR AS DAY

During *American Idol*, Scotty had the chance to sing with country star Josh Turner (*left*). He was thrilled to sing with one of his heroes!

A Singer's Life

Scotty spends many hours recording and practicing his music. As a winner of *American Idol*, he travels and attends events. But, singing live on stage is one of Scotty's favorite things.

When he is on tour, Scotty may spend months away from home. He misses Garner when he is away. But, he gets to see different cities and **perform** live concerts.

Scotty also attends events and meets fans. His fans are always excited to see him!

Scotty has been a guest on popular television and radio shows.

The week after Scotty won *American Idol*, he sang at Walt Disney World. He was also honored in a parade there!

Off the Stage

When Scotty isn't working, he spends time with friends and family. He also enjoys sports.

Scotty likes to work with groups that help people in need. Sometimes, he sings at events to raise money for special causes.

Buzz

Scotty works hard as a student and singer. He takes time away from school to work on his music **career**.

In 2012, Scotty plans to tour with country star Brad Paisley. He also plans to attend college. Fans are excited to see what's next for Scotty McCreery!

Fans often ask for Scotty's autograph.
And, reporters take his picture.

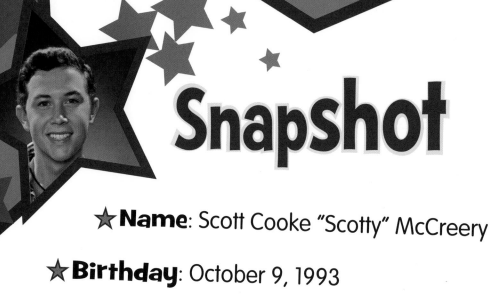

Snapshot

★ **Name**: Scott Cooke "Scotty" McCreery

★ **Birthday**: October 9, 1993

★ **Birthplace**: Garner, North Carolina

★ **Appearance**: *American Idol*

★ **Album**: *Clear As Day*

Important Words

audition (aw-DIH-shuhn) to give a trial performance showcasing personal talent as a musician, a singer, a dancer, or an actor.

career work a person does to earn money for living.

choir (KWEYE-uhr) a group of singers that perform together, usually in a church or school.

compete to take part in a contest between two or more persons or groups.

Grammy Award any of the awards given each year by the National Academy of Recording Arts and Sciences. Grammy Awards honor the year's best accomplishments in music.

guitar (guh-TAHR) a stringed musical instrument played by strumming.

musical a story told with music.

perform to do something in front of an audience.

release to make available to the public.

Web Sites

To learn more about Scotty McCreery, visit ABDO Publishing Company online. Web sites about Scotty McCreery are featured on our Book Links page. These links are routinely monitored and updated to provide the most current information available.

www.abdopublishing.com

Index

Alaina, Lauren **18**

American Idol (television show) **4, 12, 14, 15, 16, 18, 20, 22, 26, 30**

Bye Bye Birdie (musical) **10, 11**

California **16**

charity work **26**

Clarkson, Kelly **15**

Clear As Day (album) **20, 21, 30**

Cook, David **15**

education **8, 11, 15, 28**

Jackson, Randy **12, 17**

Lopez, Jennifer **12, 17**

McCreery, Ashley **6, 26**

McCreery, Judy **6, 7, 26**

McCreery, Michael **6, 7, 26**

McGraw, Tim **18**

North Carolina **6, 8, 11, 24, 30**

Paisley, Brad **28**

Presley, Elvis **8, 9, 10**

Seacrest, Ryan **12**

Turner, Josh **13, 22**

Tyler, Steven **12, 17**

Underwood, Carrie **15**